TESTIMONIES

CAST DOWN, BUT NOT DESTROYED

MARSHELL WORTHAM/HARMON

Order this book online at www.trafford.com
or email orders@trafford.com

Most Trafford titles are also available at major online book retailers.

Printed in the United States of America.

ISBN: 978-1-4269-9751-8 (sc)
ISBN: 978-1-4269-9752-5 (e)

Library of Congress Control Number: 2011917740

Trafford rev. 02/15/2012

 www.trafford.com

North America & international
toll-free: 1 888 232 4444 (USA & Canada)
phone: 250 383 6864 ♦ fax: 812 355 4082

Introduction

GOD GIVES US ALL A chance at a healthy and prosperous life. Some of us make it and some of us don't. May God be the glory for those of us who do make it. When I think about life, it puts me in the mind of a deck of playing cards. You have to know how to play your cards no matter what is dealt to you. The most important rule is simple. It's mandatory that you know your opponent's hand. You have to know how, when, and where to play your cards. Pastor Eureka Martin at Anointed Prophetic Ministries said that there is a war going on. Whether you stand up and fight or sit there, the war still goes on.

Chapter 1
From Childhood to Adulthood

THE ENEMY BEGAN TO INTERVENE in my life at an early age. His plan was to ruin my life or to just end it all together. I never understood it and could never figure out why but overcoming these obstacles became routine. Like a child just learning to ride a bicycle, I would often get up, dust myself off, and get back on the trail of life. I guess if he had his way, I would've curled up in a little knot and died. He was so wrong! When I was a child, I was tossed from home to home. This was solely due to my parents being young and inexperienced. It wasn't easy for me. Having an alcoholic father didn't help either, but one day God gave him a miracle. He saved him. He stopped him in his tracks, set him straight, and turned him around. Letting him know, there was no way he could be a productive man with all the drinking. Everyone saw the anger that was housed inside him, but I only saw my dad. The enemy tried to destroy me by giving me blow after blow. Becoming a victim of a house fire, witnessing my mother being beat on, and failing the second grade were minor incidents. Finally, we were stable in our life. We were poor, but my sisters and I never knew it. We assumed that our way of life was the natural flow of things. My mother and father were very determined. You would never hear of my father and mother begging anyone for anything. I was born in Memphis, Tennessee but spent most of my toddler years in Clarksdale, Mississippi. Shortly after, my parents moved to Senatobia, Mississippi. Moving from the projects to a trailer park was a step up for us. We moved to Matthews Trailer Park in Como Mississippi. We had one of the largest trailers in the park. Finally, everyone had their own room. We were oblivious to the struggle it took to keep the bills paid. At times, my dad would hold three jobs. I didn't care what anyone said. He was my hero. My happiness in the trailer park was short lived. At an early age, my innocence was taken from me. It wasn't broadcasted. The world didn't know. The one person that I confided in didn't believe me. That shut me up for the duration. The enemy thought he had me in a corner. Little did he know, I was a child of God. My mother took us to church every Sunday. I couldn't quite understand it, but I do remember reading that God answers prayers.

On the outside, it appeared that we were a normal family but, looks can be deceiving. No one understood how it felt to walk in another's shadow. No one knew how it felt to always be judged by another's progress or never having your own wall of fame. I'll never forget it. No one knew how much they hurt me when I graduated. Three years prior, my oldest sister graduated head of her class. You would not believe how many people from out of town showed up. I saw relatives I hadn't seen in years. No, I wasn't childish. I did not shout to the top of my voice. I never let anything negative cross my mind. It was all good. May 10, 1996 was a lonely day for me. Yes my immediate family was there but that was it. There were no out of town relatives for me. Not that I'm complaining. I've learned to adjust. My way of attending to the wound was easy. I simply added a band aid thinking that it would heal it all. So I thought. After graduation, my oldest sister suggested that I go straight to college. So, straight to college, I went. In fact, I started at the same college as she did. (Lemoyne Owen) I was thinking that things between us would be better since we were both older. I was so wrong! It was just like living at home with two mothers. It only took a half semester for me to realize that living with her and going to college was not for me. We got in a big fight. We had a few words, and ended our home away from home. There were no hard feelings from me. Things just weren't the same anymore. Although they were never "right" in the first place. But, that's another story. Matthew 27;64 Command therefore that the sepulcher be made sure until the third day, lest his disciples come by night, and still him away, and say unto the people, He is risen from the dead; so the last error shall be worse than the first. This lets me know that it has to get worse before it gets better. Better is the ending of a thing; than the beginning.

Of course, the weight of the world was on my shoulders. We were always taught to go to college. At the time, college was out for me. When I decided to go to school and work full-time, it wasn't easy. Although it seemed as if He wasn't, God was still blessing me. I was blessed to go back to school another semester. The nearest college was in Senatobia, Mississippi. This town was only fifteen minutes away. A car and money was needed quickly. With the absence of my own transportation, I attended Northwest Community College. Now that I think about it. It's really funny. The words in the bible mean exactly what it states. Hebrews 13:5 states, Let your conversation be without covetousness, and be content with such things as ye have, for he hath said, I will never leave ye, nor forsake ye. I had not yet realized His almighty power, or how He doesn't always show up when we want Him, but He's always on time. I applied for a grant just a little bit late because I thought there was no one to walk me through the process. It was the last day for admission. What I thought would take an hour or so took two to three hours. There were several tests given to me. In addition, because my financial aid was late, they surprisingly, gave me a price to attend. I still remember the amount. When I heard five hundred and eighty five dollars, I went into a daze. Every pay check there would be fifty dollars or more to come out. Not knowing the balance of my account, I left the college with my heart in my stomach. Minutes later I showed up at my bank. I was just curious. My balance was five hundred and eighty nine dollars. I didn't wait, think, or ask any questions. I immediately asked for all of the money. Changing jobs was next on my agenda. Managing to make it out with a 3.0 was even harder. My next job was at a truck stop. I broke the number one rule which was not to date a truck driver. Ignoring all the little voices that shouted no, I stood and held an hour long conversation with him. Then it was over. He had my attention and I had his number. I actually, mistakenly, took his fuel card home. After calling him to let him know he left his card. We set a date for the night. Even though I was young, I wasn't too dumb. I arranged to meet him at the job. Being the middle daughter of three girls, I was taught to take every precaution. I made my two officer friends take down his name, make and model, color, and tag number of his car. After a few times of going out, he was given the directions to my home. We hit it off, at first. All of our time was spent together. Morning, noon, and night was all about him. College slowly got pushed to the back burner. I'm sad to say, but he had turned me out. There were things that I had never experienced and places I had never been. I went and stayed a while. Sometimes the devil will take you places you really shouldn't be, and he'll make you stay longer than you intended on staying. I should've known it was something wrong. When he told me he had seven children. All of which weren't his, but one. STILL, my hands should've gone up as I walked away. Then, shortly after that little secret was out, I found out he had an anger problem. One night, after work, we went to his mother's house. His children from his marriage were there. He became so upset. He wanted me to believe there was an understanding between him and his wife. The children weren't supposed to come there anymore. I didn't understand why. He was so angry that he swung and hit a ceiling heater, busting it up. After that display rage of occurred, His son ran out to his aunt's house. He called his ex wife to come get the children. She said that she couldn't because she was attending a house party. He called her back and told her the children would be outside waiting on her. They went outside. I started to say something to him. All I was stating is that the children had shorts on. It was too cold out. He told me to shut up because this didn't have anything to do with me. The children were outside, so I joined them. Everything was cool until his ex wife showed up with a car load. She parked at the end of the drive way. Her and two or three men walked over to his aunt's house. I stood up and asked if anyone was going over to help him. No one moved, so I grabbed a plank and walked over. I was a 4'11" college student, but I was about to show them who was really boss. Fortunately, no one got crazy and everyone went home. Just when everyone was about to go to bed, her husband came, stood, and shot up in the air. I had no idea how much trouble I was in but someone called my dad. Now, let me be the first to tell you. No one messes with his daughters. He came to rescue me. All of the drama got me so upset and no one wanted that, because I was four months pregnant. Being young and dumb, I didn't recognize he was running from responsibility. Some people may think they can run pretty fast. You may even out run a bullet but you can never out run God. It was moving day for us. The apartment complex we lived in was perfect. It was a little expensive but perfect. We didn't have everything we wanted but that was okay. There was a small black and white television. It played out eventually. We only had a bed, a few dishes, and some clothes. Soon God allowed us to get living room furniture. Later, my mother and father gave us a kitchen table from which they purchased at rummage sale. Of course, I didn't mind. It's hard being choosey when you don't have any money. It was difficult, but I was willing to suffer for love. The neighborhood we stayed in was good. It was perfect for a young, single, and pregnant woman. At the time, I was thinking that it was destiny that got me where I was. Little did I know, I was only living above my means. Most of the time, it's easily mistaken. I was still traveling from Southaven to Senatobia for work and suddenly it came to a halt. It got much harder. Rent was seven hundred and thirty five dollars, electricity, gas, grocery, and other necessities of life were just a little too much. The end of our lease was nearing and we both knew what we had to do. We started searching for a new place early. Thinking the perfect place was found, the moving process started. It seemed wonderful because it was down the road from my job, and around the corner from the babysitter. The apartment was viewed in a timely manner. Whenever she had us to look at the town house it was in the evening. In other words, only enough light to see how to get around. It looked bigger than the last place, but not as good. That was okay. I made sure I walked through twice. Finally, move in date was there. My mom, dad, and uncle helped us move in. It was quick. I quickly recognized some potential thieves. However, I prayed and moved on I believed God would protect and keep me where ever I stayed. I never shared my concerns with anyone. When everyone finally left it was in the day time. I opened the door, walked in, and jumped in the first kitchen chair I found. Roaches were crawling everywhere. The baby's father and I decided to go to Wal-Mart to pick up some things to make the house feel like a home. We spent over two hundred dollars on items to terminate any pests or rodents. Rolling up our sleeves, we were determined to overcome this obstacle. Finally, I had to admit my defeat. I stood firmly in the middle of the floor and shouted to the top of my voice. "We can't stay here! I will not bring my son into this place!" Since we still had ownership of the old apartment keys, we packed up the mattress and went back. Due to the apartment being in my name, I was left to handle the hard work. The apartment manager and I talked. She let me know that we had not held to the obligation of our lease. Since it appeared that we were tied to this lease we decided to stay while we searched for something else. It only took one day, so I don't understand why it was such a problem to get our money back. The lady who showed us the place wasn't cooperating so I demanded to speak to the manager. She told me she couldn't give me all my money back. First, I was told there wasn't any money. Then the story changed and I was given the option to get my money, but not my deposit. The baby's father was okay with it, but I was not trying to hear that. Why not, I thought. We hadn't lived there yet. Now that I think back, each time we viewed the apartment we were rushed through the visit. It was always in the evening time. The infestation problem wasn't announced. I wanted my money. She said no. I turned and said, "Tomorrow, you will have a visit from channel 5 news. You may steal my money, but no one else's." I left. The next day I showed up. A few minutes later, channel 5 news rolled up behind me. As I entered the door, the manager met me. She handed me the money with no questions asked. I came out waving the money. The anchor man smiled and said, "Glad to be of service to you." I never thought to bow down and give God a sincere thank you. Again, moving on began to be a natural thing for me. God was making a way out of no way and truly blessing me. Upon moving into the next apartment, we were blessed to learn that the baby's father's best friend lived across the street. At that time, my oldest sister was babysitting for me. Soon, she started giving me grief. The best friend's girl friend, at the time, felt sorry for me. She offered to take care of my son until I got off from work. That was right up my alley. One night around Christmas, it started to snow. I was working at J C Penny. I loved my job. I became comfortable and layed back. Well, they had this policy. No one could leave until their shift was completely over. I knew the policy, but I assumed that they would understand should I have to leave. When all the customers started to leave because of the snow, I decided to wait it out. The snow didn't let up and no customers came. I asked my supervisor if I could leave. He acted as if I said nothing. I waited little longer and by this time I was furious. I walked straight into the manager's office. I told her that I had a new born baby several miles away at the babysitter. This seemed to have no affect on her at all. I'm just like my father. I've always been told showing a person is better than telling them. So, I got up, walked out of her office and never looked back. I put caution to the wind. Instead of turning left at the end of the hallway, I turned right. I walked straight out the door. I got into my car, and headed to pick up my son. Guess what? When I got there, he wasn't there. I drove across town to the babysitter's mother house. No one was there. By this time, I am beginning to get upset. I drove back to the babysitter's house. Finally, he was there. I hugged him like he had been kidnapped. All I could think about was my little man. I never thought about the fact that I had never driven in snow. Once I got home, it finally dawned on me. My son and I had bonded. We had become mother and child. I must admit. It did take me a little while longer than others. I was young, dumb, and stupid. Following an older man was my main goal at that time. God had to let me fall flat on my face to see that He was my "sugar daddy."

The last straw was broken the day of a friend's wedding. We weren't childhood friends but we were associates. This was wonderful time for them but a bad time for us. Nonetheless, I accepted since they asked me to be in their wedding. One day we were at home doing our thing. He thought he was so good. He expected me to fall off to sleep right after. He jumped up and put on his basketball clothes, kissed me on the cheek, and whispered in my ear, "I'm going to play ball." It didn't bother me because I was not trying to be the clinging type. Then something told me to follow him. It took me about thirty minutes to put my clothes on. I drove to the same park he always played at. I convinced myself this was stupid. I've always went with him to play. He's never lied. That was just it. I wasn't with him. Why did he all of a sudden want to go without me? I had to see for myself. I got to the park. This park has about eight to ten goals on the court. I was surprised. I Got out and walked to every last single goal. He was nowhere to be found. I was getting hotter and hotter as I drove off. I spotted my car. It was in front of the police station. This was yards from the basketball court. If it was a snake it would've bitten me. That wasn't enough. Being the detective I was, I wanted to make sure that this was my car. Looking on the inside was my next step. After finding everything intact, I shut the car door, planted my but on the trunk and waited. It began to get late and the sun started to set. Finally, I realized that the police station wasn't the place to act a fool. I went home with all these crazy thoughts racing through my mind. My eyes were swollen from all the tears that I rubbed from my face. Finally he decided to show up. I grabbed a butcher knife and met him at the door. He thought I was joking. I demanded answers and began to shout to the top of my voice. It felt as though time had stood still. Everything went in slow motion. I smashed his Playstation and all his games to make it clear I was serious. It was soon time for the wedding rehearsal. The bride and groom knew something was wrong because we didn't say two words to each other. We somehow made it through the rehearsal and were able to remain cordial to one another. On the way home, I started up again. In the middle of traffic, I lost it. Grabbing the steering wheel while he was driving was the farthest I had ever gone. There was a rehearsal dinner at the bride's mother's house. I only attended to be polite. No one said anything to me. Feeling all out of place, tears began to flow. He brought me home and lied. He told me he left something over their house. He'd be right back. I stayed up and waited. It got later and later. I finally went to bed with all kinds of thoughts running through my mind. I woke up the next morning and I didn't know whether to worry or be angry. After searching the apartment, I found that most of his clothes were gone. That really didn't mean much because he lived out of his truck anyway. I walked through the living room and saw that his Playstation was gone. That gave me my answer. I quickly hurried off to his best friend's house. I banged on the door. No one came. I knew he was there. My car was in the street. I raced back home to get the rest of his stuff. As I came down the stairs, a fine young man was going in his apartment. He stopped and asked with a concerned look on his face. "Is anything wrong?" With tears running down, I said, "Nothing, I just need to do some spring cleaning." Then he turned around, walked towards me and said, "Is that something I could help you with?" I told him no. This was something that I had to do alone. Although it would have been so easy to take him up on his offer, cheating was not a part of my character. After packing all of his worthless pictures from the wall, I later played target practice in the back yard of his best friend's house with some of his things. Then, I drove to Mississippi and spent the night with my parents. That turned out to be a very restless night. The wedding was the next day. No one really expected me to show up. They could've cared less if I did or didn't. We acted like nothing had gone wrong between us. Once again, we were very cordial. After the wedding, he went one way and I went the other. Like a bug in a brown paper bag, I was lost when I came home from the wedding. It was just me, my son, and an empty apartment. Later on, the baby's father showed up. Like any mad couple, few words were passed. He stayed in the bathroom and cut his hair. Usually, when he cuts his hair, he cuts my son's as well. That was the last thing he did. He slowly walked through the living room and said he had to go. I expected him to walk back through. A minute or two passed by. I got up and looked out the door. My car was nowhere to be found. I immediately went to the pay phone and called him. He didn't answer. I knew that he could not be too far ahead so I jumped on the interstate and raced after him. I finally caught up with him. I began to blink my lights on and off and he finally pulled over. We argued for a few minutes. Then I lost it. I forced him to take the baby with him. I drove off, never looking back. I was so angry. I made to my parents house in less than five minutes. No one knew I was even there. It didn't even feel right. I was restless. My heels couldn't cool. I jumped up and drove to Batesville. Although I knew how to get to the house, I still got lost. God had to put me in an unfamiliar place. So many things were jumping in and out of my head. When I came to myself, I was in Tunica. During the drive back to my parent's house, I calmed down. My stay there wasn't long. Again, my heels couldn't cool. Back to Batesville I went. This time my car was there. I didn't waste any time. I burst through the doors, spoke, picked up my son, and walked right out of the house. They all stopped, as if, they had seen a ghost. I placed my son's car seat on the passenger side, strapped him in, and promptly drove off. His father was lucky that he was not closer or he would have been as good as run over. God had to save me. I was so deep in love that I could not see nor think straight. That wasn't me. I've never fought over men. It's too many in the sea. This one had my heart completely and totally. As I drove back to Como, his grandmother's house got further and further away in my rear view mirror. I don't remember how it went, but I told my father and mother I was home to stay. I felt like the prodigal son returning home to his father. They looked relieved. A big weight was lifted. I took a breath, got into bed and snuggled closely with my son beside me. Tears began to roll down my face as I remembered the words that I said when I left. "When I leave, I'm never coming back." If no one else but my parents, at least they were happy. The next morning they stood in the door peeking in. They smiled as they watched me as I slept with my head layed on my son's chest.

The dust finally settled and all the fog cleared. However, the relationship was still unbreakable. At least that's what I wanted to believe. Months and months went by. No calls, no pictures, no letters, and no telegrams. Nothing. Finally, a big box of clothes for my son came. You know I smiled from ear to ear. Shortly after, a call came. I fussed and cried like it was no tomorrow. He told some sweet lie about losing his job, and I let him back in. He helped me out every now and then. The two car notes were mine. Even though, he lied like he was going to help me with them. They were in my name. They were my pocket's responsibility. The world says love is blind. Well, lust is just as blind. We went back and forth for years. My son loved the father that I reminded him of having. There were birthdays and Christmases he missed. Every now and then, I let my son go alone with his father but when the weight of the world was too much to bear, I jumped in too. I saw states I'd never seen. That's why I tell anybody not to run from their problems. No matter how fast or far you run. You can never run away from your problems. When you get back, the same problem you ran from will stare you dead in the face.

At this point, my son was three years old. I was still trying to hold on to something not worth holding on to. Every blue moon he would drop in town, He had my son trained. He would get excited when he heard the sound of an eighteen wheeler. I'm ashamed to admit it but I did too. The last draw was simple for me. I have never had a man to put his hands on me. I'll tell you why after I explain what happened. I had been spending a lot of time over his mother's house. No one knew, but a lot of things were going through my mind. There were two cars. It was one person paying the car note. He had a good paying job. After all, he was a truck driver. Guess what? I had the brand new car. He had the old one. He drove to work in it like it was his own. It made me mad as hell. One day he decided to take his grandmother downtown. I put my foot down and demanded that he take the other car. That made him mad. You can't let everybody use you as a door mat forever. That was my gas in the other car. He wasn't going to just run it out. You know he gave some lame excuse about the car being too small. Then he made me get in the back. I understood that his grandmother was old so she needed to sit in the front. I pulled the seat forward for her to sit in the back. She raised her voice at me and told me she wasn't going to sit in the back because she couldn't. You know that made me even more upset. Then he made some comment to me as if I were a child. I hardly ever rode in the car. A car that I was paying the note on, putting gas in, and washing yet I have to ride in the back seat. We rode to the town of Batesville. I was sitting in the car the whole time full of anger, never letting it go. I could've blown it up with those two still in it. We got a little rowdy as we left the parking lot. I asked him to turn the radio up. He hardly moved it. I reached up front and turned it up myself. He turned it back down. Somehow, while reaching up to move it again, I was thrown to the back roughly. My hand ended up on the side of his face on purpose. The ride back to his mother's house was not pleasant. I stormed through the doors in a rage. My soul purpose was to damage something of his. I walked over to his play station and started stumping on it. He grabbed me and slammed me in the middle of the floor. All I saw was red. Not stopping, it continued. He body slammed me again; this time on the sofa. It was evident he didn't love me. Anybody with a half a brain wouldn't do that. The sofa didn't have any pillows. It was made up of wood and cover. Now that I think back, he could've easily broken my back. I jumped up and ran in the bath room. The window was held up by a wooden stick. I snatched it down and began to swing. Crazy and out of my mind, I swung and broke the bath room window. He flung the door open and headed towards me. The bathroom was too small to fight in. I came out swinging. Because he was such a big man, he took the stick and broke it like it was a twig. Again, he body slammed me in the kitchen floor. His grandmother called me by my nick name and said, "Chu—Chu, why don't you stay down?" Yelling in anger, I said, "Why don't you call the police?" Then I spotted the phone, so I called. I ended up hanging up before I talked to anyone. They were already on their way. At this time, my son was bare foot and in a pamper. He hardly ever spoke, but he could understand everything you said. I told him to go get in the car. The police did not do anything when they arrived. The town of Batesville is so close knit. Everyone is related to someone or knows someone. His cousin came out to the house. He threatened to call Child Protective Service on me. I, in return said, "On what grounds? You aint talking to no fool. I know my rights." Then they told me I had to leave. I agreed, but I wanted my car keys to the other car. The baby's father began to look like a fool. Then he said that wasn't my car. The police still insisted that I leave. The police said that I couldn't drive two cars at one time. I could clearly see I was fighting a losing battle. Even after being shown the car note with the car in my father's name. They still weren't convinced. I drove off. Once I got down the road, I looked in the glove compartment and found what I was looking for. I immediately turned around. The police officers were following me just to see if I would come back. I slowed down to show them the title to my car. When I got back pity was riding my back. I didn't take the car keys. Graduation rehearsal was an hour away. The rest of the night was spent begging him to forgive me and to come to my graduation. One of the most proud moments of my life was ruined. Even though I was tired, continuing my education was one of my top priorities.

I didn't realize it but getting a new job became normal. I didn't recognize the spirits that had attached themselves to me. Being around someone who never handled his responsibilities or kept a job had grown on me. Sometimes you can do more harm to yourself than drugs itself. After graduation, Horseshoe Casino was my next move. Of course, that was not in God's plan. From the moment I stepped in to the moment I left. I stayed sick. I went from Senatobia Children's Clinic to Liberty National Insurance. If someone really took the time to look at it, they would have found that God was still blessing me. Times got so hard. I was admitted to North Oak Regional Hospital. I remember being in the E R. It must have been pretty bad because everyone called my pastors. I remember the doctor telling me

I was regurgitating the lining of my stomach. I applied for a job at the IRS and received a timely response which was surprising to me. The bad part about it was they called while I was still in the hospital. No one knew where I was because I refused to tell anyone. The IRS wanted to know how long I would be in the hospital. It's funny how that worked out because I was being discharged that day. After resting a day, I went straight in to work. The job was seasonal, but it lasted for a year and a half. The baby's father wasn't there, but God was still blessing me. I never knew why. No one could ever explain it to me. People have always disliked me for no reason. I could be the nicest person on earth and I still would have been hated. I met this nice guy while working at the IRS. We hit it off from the beginning. There was this other lady, Jonathan, and myself. We would always hang out and eat lunch together. The three of us always talked about God. It was funny to me their perception of God and salvation. I convinced him to come to my church. Being proud of my church, I spoke of it all the time. Even though, I was not willing to lay my sinful ways down at the time. There was a battle with my spiritual man and my flesh. Coming from the church I did, "Sunday Christianity" was normal for me. Of course, we ended our friendship. He was much younger than I. Our minds were in two different places but I don't regret meeting him. He was a real gentleman. One night it was storming and I was scared to drive to Mississippi. He made me follow him home and I slept over his house. When I say gentleman, I mean gentleman. He kissed me good night and closed the door to his bed room. His mother and father raised a good young man, and I thank them. The second time he came to my church was surprising. He sat two rows behind me. That's the day my car quit on the interstate. Most people would've gone back home, but I knew where my help was. That Sunday the Apostle Eric Martin ministered to me. I can remember him telling me God wanted me to be alone, for now. After church, Jonathan gave me my key back to my apartment. Oh, yeah, I had moved out of my parent's house. My dad was scared to let me go home after work, so he made me stay overnight sometimes even though I was grown enough to live alone. Still young and scared, most of my time was spent at my parent's house. Sometimes we ask for things all bold. We have no idea the fight we will have to go through to get or keep them.

At this point, my birthday was coming up. I was determined to have some fun. There was this guy constantly bugging me to go out. Not listening to the voices on the inside, we went out. Now that I think about it, everyone laughed when they heard about my date. It wasn't about me dating. It was who I was dating. Determined to find a good man, I had to learn that it's not the woman's job to find someone. She is to be found. Proverbs 18:22 reads, He who finds a wife finds a good thing and obtains favor from the LORD. So, you women need to stop looking. We went out. He was smooth, but something was definitely wrong. There was a true battle going on with my flesh. Being a bible reader, I would read my bible before going to bed. One night I was reading the bible before turning in. Now, take in consideration that I am a dreamer. That means that God deals with me through dreams. I'm not announcing the gift of prophesy but I do realize prophecy is there. Now, back to my dream. I got up to go to bed, closed the bible, locked the door, and using the bathroom always came next. As I slept, this is what I dreamed. I got up to use the bathroom. When you come out of the bathroom, the kitchen is to the right. After drinking a cup of water, I was walking back to bed. Then a little voice said, "Read me." I turned to pick up my bible. Remember, my bible is closed. Asking God to let me turn to whatever pertains to me, I opened it to verses about divorce. It was stating that you couldn't marry another for the sake of sex alone. Matthew 5:32 reads, But I say to you that everyone who divorces his wife, except on the ground of sexual immorality, makes her commit adultery, and whoever marries a divorced woman commits adultery. Not understanding, I rushed off to bed. Not too much longer I was up. Still dreaming, I went to the bath room. As I was leaving, I got some water. After my water, again, little voices began to speak. "Read me," was what I heard. You know I went over to read. Once again, I told God to let me turn it to the place I needed to read. This time I opened it on this certain scripture.

Proverbs 18:22 which reads, A man that findeth a wife findeth a good thing and obtains favor in the Lord. I began to laugh and get happy. I asked God what He was trying to tell me. I went back to bed and continued my dream. Once again, I dreamt that I rose to use the bathroom. While sitting on the toilet, a sick feeling came over me. I quickly pulled the tub's curtain back. There was a dark shaped figure in the tub. As I walked out the bathroom, it followed me. I went to my bed room and sat on the bed, Afraid to get under the covers. I pulled them back. Then the black figure turned into the guy I went out with. No one knows this, but my son has always been my little guardian angel. He came in and sat on the floor, and crossed his legs as he watched television. He turned his back to us and began to watch a television that has never been in my room. The presence of my son made this guy uneasy. He got up and left. Psalms 1:5 reads, Therefore the wicked will not stand in the judgment, nor sinners in the assembly of the righteous. The crazy thing about it was that he walked through the wall. He didn't leave out the front door. That dream scared me to death. Days later, we were talking. Out of the blue, my mouth opened and words came from my soul. I confronted him with something I really didn't know but felt like I knew. I was telling him about my dream. Then I explained my dream even though I really didn't understand it myself, I opened my mouth and this is what came out. Once I told him of my dream. I asked him if he was married. Act 2:17 And in the last days it shall be, God declares, that I will pour out my Spirit upon all flesh, and your sons and your daughters shall prophesy, and your young men shall see visions, and your old men shall dream dreams: He asked me why? Then I told him how God deals with me. He got so mad. He said that someone was in his business and stormed out. He started stalking me. I was young and frightened so my parent's house became my residence. One night, I came home and the house was different. Someone had cleaned up and fixed me dinner. The gesture would've been perfect if whomever had a key. I went straight to my parent's house. I was already shaken up and then I received a disturbing telephone call from the baby's father. I called my pastor. She was ministering to me over the phone.

Then she said, "You need to be right here for me to talk to you."
I immediately asked my mother if I could use her car to go to
Batesville. When I arrived, they stopped everything to talk to
me. The apostle was having a men moment with some of the
new members. He does that. He's great at it. Anyway, they sat
me down at the table and began to talk. I explained the dream,
how my son would never leave us alone, and how someone got
into my apartment. They helped me to understand how my son
saw something that I didn't see. That wasn't the first time he
would disturb us. Whenever the guy was over, my son would
always stay up. I'd put him to bed and he would wake up and sit
on the floor beside the sofa. That made me think. Hebrews 13:2
reads, Be not forgetful to entertain strangers: for thereby some
have entertained angels unawares. After talking for a while,
easing my nerves, and remembering who I served. I was ready
to humble my little self and let Him fight my battles. As I was on
my way out the door, a new member asked me if I could drop
him off at home. Well, I thought to myself, that wasn't the way I
was going, but I would be glad to give him a ride.

Like I said before, people should be careful in asking God
for things. Sometimes God will give you exactly what you ask
for. No one tells you what you have to go through to get it. No
one tells you what you have to go through to keep it. I'm almost
certain. No one told you of all the spirits that come along with
whatever you begged God for.

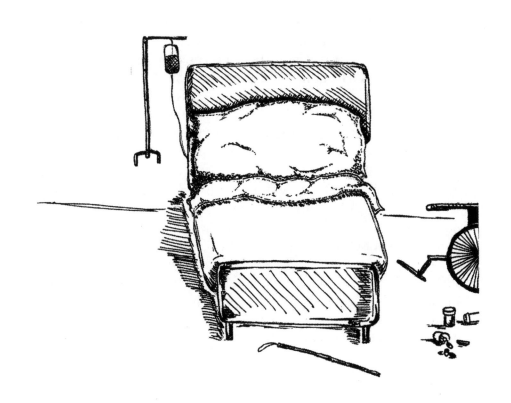

Chapter 2
Stripped of Everything

My next few testimonies are strictly for the single and lonely. Be extra careful who you let in your home and heart. This chapter of this book is short and simple. Just like the situation was. That night I dropped the new member off at home. As we drove across town, we began to talk. He seemed like a nice guy. Our conversation was pleasant and subtle. He asked if I was doing anything the upcoming weekend. I began to think before I answered. I rationalized the pending acceptance of the offer by telling myself this was the best time to treat myself to nice company. Then I thought to myself, I thought he and Shay-Shay were dating. Whether it was a lie or not did not matter to me. I was told not to worry about it. I didn't. I am the type of person who stays in her own business. So, I wouldn't know if someone specifically came out and told me a lie. The day came for our little outing or date if you will. My youngest sister came over to fix my hair. This was a special time for me because I hadn't dated for a while. He didn't have a car so his sister and her new husband went with us. It was lovely because I admired his sister. The next day he came over. Once again, we departed late. I noticed he was coming over three nights in a row. I didn't mind. My pastor always talked with me due to my struggle with my fleshly desires. Trust me single individuals. If you are having a hard time alone, don't rush into another relationship. It's a reason why God has you alone. Maybe He's preparing you for your mate. Or maybe He's preparing your mate for you. It's true what the bible says. The spirit is always willing to do that which is right in the eyes of the Lord but the flesh is weak. You can profess as much as you want about what you are not going to do anymore. Truth be told, if you haven't been delivered from that particular spirit you will back slide every time. That's just what I did. One night he came over and I was cooking dinner. My son even opened up to him and everything which was rare. He usually clams up with everyone. I happened to look in the other room. My son wouldn't stop talking. I figured that was a plus on his part. Then it was the food test. I let him taste my cooking. He liked it. I wasn't aware that he was a wonderful cook. When God puts something together, He makes no mistakes. That night one thing led to another. We got caught up in the moment. It was over. He never left. Sleeping with different guys was one thing, but this was different. Even though it was done a few times more, we both genuinely felt bad. Instead of waiting for him to pop the question, I pushed him to do the right thing. I wasn't going to be another hit and quit it victim. Well, I wouldn't say push him. I simply mentioned to him that we can't be sleeping together and unwed. Either we were going to do the right thing or stop. My response was, "Yeah, I know." A month later it was done. Our church took a trip to Georgia. We didn't sleep together but we spent most of our time with one another. Shay-Shay was there. There wasn't any bad blood between us so I proceeded with the relationship. I had no idea of the talk that was going on behind my back. We didn't waste any time because of this simple fact. I thought everything was fine. I began to talk to God as I became worried about the situation. I wanted to know what He had to say. After God told me this was who He had for me, I proceeded. I never asked was it too soon or should I wait just a little while longer. See, sometimes God has someone for you but He may not be finished with him or her. Some things are only meant for a season. When that season is up, God removes it. Hearing clearly from God, my mind was made up. There was a old lady in Georgia who confirmed it all. She didn't know me. I didn't know her. It was the part of the service when prophecy came. The apostle hadn't said a word. He likes to let you make your own mind up when it comes to relationships. First, this old lady pulled me to the side. She whispered in my ear, "You don't believe he loves you. You are capable of being loved. Trust God. He sent him. He really loves you and your son" I say again. She had never seen him or me. She didn't even know how he looked. What came out of her mouth was from God. Then on top of that, the apostle grabbed me and ministered to me. He told me exactly what was on my mind. I know he hears directly from God. "You're worried about whether you are doing the right thing. You're worried about what people say. Don't worry. He's God sent." That night I was amazed. I'd begun to think that I was cursed. Every man I had ever found left. That's the key words. I found. That's why I tell any female this. You may know he's the one. God may have already confirmed it to you. Wait. The scripture reads the way it does for a reason. Moving only a second too soon will mess you up. Trust me. It will be worth the wait. Don't get me wrong. You will have problems, but you shouldn't add to them.

My whole family was either mad or shocked. First, I didn't ask anyone. Second, he wasn't my type. Here's why I did it that way. When I made the move to marry, I asked the confirmation of one individual. I know it's tradition to ask the father or mother for their blessing but what if they don't approve? Will you still go through with it? Should you still go through with it? Everyone could clearly see he wasn't my type. I'm use to tall, good-looking, well established, educated, saved, and older men. At that point in time, I really wasn't concerned with all of that stuff. He may have had one thing going for himself. He was much taller than I. Where he worked, there wasn't a lot of money. He was younger than I was so you know he didn't have any money saved. He looked okay but not a prince. Then on top of that, he dropped out of school. My car needed to be fixed so there was no vehicle and he did not own one. I know all you Christians think I'm just bad mouthing him. Just give me a chance to explain. God was taking me down a journey I'd never been on before. I noticed his desire to make it in spite of his circumstances. He had a humble spirit. He has the kind of spirit that will leave you standing alone, arguing with yourself, and feeling real foolish. One Friday afternoon, I had called my parents. They were to pick me up to wash clothes at their house. I was under the impression that he was going along with me to meet the family. At the last minute, he changed his mind. We had our first disagreement. I went on without him. Now that I think about it. He really tried to stay around and wait on me. He called my parents house about two or three times. Of course, I was still mad. I fussed as I folded his clothes. My little arms were tired at the end of the night. When I got back home later on that night, surprisingly, no one was there. Once he came in, I played it smart. My son had his own room and bed yet I placed him in the bed with me. He was ready for bed, but read between the lines. He quietly got in my son's bed. Full of anger, I turned the light on. Stood in my son's door and began to preach. I stayed there so long. He got up and went to the living room. I guess it was too much for him because he went outside to smoke a cigarette. After smoking, he came back in. Then I smelled liquor. I stood firmly with my hands on my hips and said, "If this is what you are bringing to the table, you can keep it. I don't need someone who drinks. My mother put up with it for years, but not me. I chose you for a reason. We can end it now with no hard feelings. I can get any bum off the street. I thought you were ready for a change." He was quiet so I know he was listening. Then I asked him if he wanted me to help him get his GED. He answered me as if he got offended, so I left it alone. We never really had a real conversation about what we wanted. I can remember explaining to him, but he never expressed how he felt. He never complained or objected. On November 27, 2003 at 7:00 p.m., we got married. As I look back, there were certain things that could've upset me, but I refused to be down. My best friend totally forgot. She works a lot so I understood. Then I thought it had something to do with my type of church. She has never come when I invited her, but that's okay. My mother in law wasn't there. Her excuse was that she didn't receive an invitation. Yeah right. No one else did either, but that was okay. Then I noticed my little sister wasn't acting the same. No one was ruining my night. I mean no one. Even my son was mean mugging me. I knew what that was all about. Instead of my husband, he wanted his dad. Well, I got married on a Friday. I was admitted to the hospital on Monday. These are the testimonies that really mean a lot to me. They're not just words simply rolling off my tongue or thoughtless memories floating around in my past. I give God praise at the thought of what could've, should've, or would've happened. Monday my friend Mary Norwood was trying to find me a doctor to go to. I didn't have much money or any insurance. She ended up taking me to her husband's doctor. They were out for lunch, so we had to come back. From then on I have no recollection of what happened next. When I opened my eyes, I was laying in a hospital bed. My new husband was right by my side. I can't recall the length of time I was there either. All I know is that I was in a size 3/4 and loved it. It's like I blinked my eyes and I blew up. Unaware of what was going on, the doctor in the emergency room caught my attention. No, it wasn't his looks. Even though, he was very good looking. I was now married. I guess it was the way he handled me and my diabetes. He didn't treat me like I was a lab rat. He sounded like he knew what he was talking about and he got me in and out of there. Little did I know, the doctor's office was forty-five minutes away. I went anyway. My husband knew the doctor was good looking to me. I never got out of place or crazy so he let it slide. My husband and I only shared a few weeks together without tears. I had been layed off from IRS. My unemployment benefits were only one hundred and forty-five dollars a week. God was still blessing. My rent was three hundred and eighty seven dollars a month. I've never been too crazy with money. My father and mother taught me well. After saving up my checks for three weeks, I only had forty dollars left. Groceries and cleaning supplies were bought with that. That was before I got married. I thought that I would have help with a husband. I became worried when it didn't go the way I had dreamed. One thing God did bless me with was a man that knew how to handle money. On a scale from one to ten, he scored off the charts. Then there was this idea of us moving to the projects. I rejected that idea first hand. My car was down, so my mother and I were together. I was handling my business with her. Somehow we were on the sidewalk of an ophthalmologist. As I walked down the sidewalk, this voice began to speak to me. Being that I had already been wanting to go to the eye doctor. I went inside. They gave me an appointment. The appointment came and I went. Another doctor saw me. Then my main doctor saw me. Three or four doctors were in the room at one time. I thought to myself. Something must be wrong. It's too many professional people in one room at one time. All you heard was whispering. I said, "Anything wrong?" They quickly said, "Nothing, we're just going to let this eye specialist from Oxford take a look at your eyes. Although I had no knowledge of what they saw, fear never reared its head. The appointment for Oxfords appointment was made. I literally walked in blind as a bat. They didn't make it any better. All they said was my vision was leaving. Little did I know, it was already gone in one eye. Fear still didn't rear its head. I guess I had more faith than I really realized. I didn't have a problem until the doctors started finding stuff. I didn't realize God had been talking to me all the time. Weeks before I applied for disability, I was visiting my parent's house. I opened my mail. There was a letter from social security. Unfortunately, they denied my request. Heartbroken as I was, determination was my fuel. It wasn't like I was lying. At this point, I was legally blind. The hard part wasn't that I was going blind. It wasn't that I was a new wife, or that I was still young. It was the fact that my son was a young child. He still had to be raised. If I didn't work, who would? Before I even knew of being legally blind, God had me reading my bible like a flowing river. It was like I was hungry for something. Day in and day out, I would read. Being married was pushing me into another place. Fighting an anger spirit isn't easy when you're grown up in hatred. With everything that I was going through, I prayed like never before. The new neighborhood, home, in-laws and family were taking me through. I cried for days after moving in. I'd never seen floors that were supposed to be cleaned but looked so bad. None of the rooms had a true closet with doors. After having my pity party, I sucked it up. At this time, I was learning how to pray. That's one thing about God. He'll give you what you ask Him for. I sincerely asked Him for discernment. Hearing everyone talk about it, I asked God for the ability to see spirits with my natural eyes. It's true. God reigns on the just and the unjust. He's faithful in His word. Are you faithful in yours? In His word it says, "God has no respective person." That means God can bless who He wants to bless. Even the ones you think don't deserve it. That's why people should watch who they talk about. I had to learn to smile and laugh while people stood with a knife waiting to stab me. Some of the holiest people kill every day with their tongue, but that's another story.

My treatment started with eye drops. After that didn't seem to help, more tests came. They ventured further. I remember having only one operation in Oxford. They attempted to remove the cataracts. Happiness came, because it actually did some good. Unfortunately, it didn't last long. On top of all that, I was dealing with a sperm donor. Yes, he had been demoted. He was no longer a father. He had never been a dad. I tried to make someone be dad and he didn't know the first thing about it. Extensive surgery was done on my eyes. When my blood pressure began to elevate, they transferred me to Memphis. Coming to terms with losing my eyesight was not an easy task. I had to step out of my comfort zone and learn to love someone else besides the sperm donor. My family not only was pushed to the side. They were isolated. I'm use to going to family functions, family trips, and family outings. Before they shipped me off to Memphis, I was approved for disability. My husband was moving from temporary job to temporary job. That's when I really learned to pray. I'm use to making a way for myself. Depending on others was not my style. God had to make me humble. He had to put me in a place where I couldn't call on mommy and daddy for everything. This was uncomfortable, but I was determined to stick it out. I remember one day. I got so tired of my upstairs being dirty. Down stairs was okay.

Everybody had to see that, so we kept it clean. I did nothing. Clothes and trash just piled up around me. Trust me. I tried. So, I went from my son's room to my room, cleaning. That's not easy for a blind person. My walk was deteriorating which caused my balance to be off too. I had this straw, dirty clothes hamper. It was in the closet empty. I nicely put all the clothes inside. Guess what? My husband, thoughtlessly, got out of his clothes and left them right beside the hamper. I was already mad, because no one thought once about the hard work I'd done. The clothes beside the hamper weighed heavy on my brain. I was trying so hard to be submissive and keep my mouth closed. I picked the hamper up and walked it to the room next door. Instead of going to the next room, I went a little farther. As I bent over to place the hamper in the room, I found no floor. It was too late. The basket fell to the bottom of the stairs, and I came tumbling after. I hit my head so hard. My body ached so badly. I just laid there. Everyone came running out of their rooms. My husband rushed down to pick me up. While my son stood at the top of the stairs crying, as if, he thought I was dead. After my husband sat me on the bed, I searched my body to see if anything was broken. I slowly walked to my son's room to let him know I was fine. He was still crying. My son gave me a hug that was out of this world. The emergency room was never thought of. A few days later I realized there was damage. My memory wasn't all there. They took me to the hospital. They didn't want to deal with me for reasons I'll explain later. I woke up in a dark room. I didn't understand why everyone still had the blinds shut. I said to my mother, "Ma, why is it so dark in here? Why yall still got the blinds closed?" My mom, being a praying mother, said they were opened. I began to cry when I finally realized what she was saying. Not only that. The reason the hospital refused me service was because I was now a renal patient. With everything that happened to me, it's hard to keep all the events in order. I just give God praise for my mind. The reason for all the swelling was my kidneys. I thank God for the doctor that looked so good. He instantly knew what it was. I like the way doctors run their practice. They may know the problem. If they don't specialize in that field, they won't diagnose anything. My first visit was scary. The doctor was a female. She didn't waste any time. My Diabetes Specialist sent over my blood work. She walked in and broke it all down. I shed a few tears and sucked it up. It took me a little while to come back to reality. There was no time for a pity party. There were no choices to be made. An appointment was made to put the catheter in my chest. That was scary. Once the catheter was in, I was okay. Everything was cool until I found out what really happens to my body once on the machine. Take into consideration a catheter doesn't last for long. I had to have surgery to have a shunt placed in my arm. Two more catheters were inserted in my chest, while my arm healed. I've always had a fear of doctors and needles. Going through over the years of my life, I learned that having fear is a sin. You're not trusting in God when you let fear take over your life. Shouldn't you trust God to protect you? If He does let something happen to you, it's for the best. Whether it's to punish, chastise, or bless you. It's all for the best. How can you be chastised if you don't know how, when, or where you went wrong? The bible says He chastises the ones He loves. Our parents punish us for doing wrong. Not because they love to see us in pain or hurt. They do it to teach us not to do it again. God is just like your natural parents. He is your father. If His word says not to do something today, it means the same thing tomorrow.

My purpose of mentioning all of this is to let you know I've been through a lot. Being converted didn't happen overnight. People may tell you loving God makes it easy. Wrong! He may be your motivation or coach for getting or staying saved, but that doesn't make it easy. See, when you were in the world. You were one of the devil's best workers. You did your job to the best of your ability. He's not going to let you go just like that. Once you get a clue of why you're still here and who makes it all possible, the devil becomes angry. He's not worried about who he has tricked. I just want you to know that a true deliverance is not pretty. Everyone wants one. Are you willing to go through the process to get delivered? Most people don't want to wait on a true deliverance to take place. The devil himself will pay you a personal house visit in the process. Not to scare you. Have no fear. God always has your back. The reason for mentioning this is because of the way people treated me. I knew I was dealing with an anger demon. The first step in deliverance is recognizing the spirit. Second, you must sincerely ask God to help you with it. Ask God to be delivered. Third, people must give you time to be delivered. They just have to stand back and watch the fireworks. My reason for saying that is this. The devil himself will come out. Deliverance isn't pretty. I continued to stay sick. At one point in time, my hands and feet were affected with neuropathy. It got so bad. I made an appointment at my diabetes doctor. He gave me some pain pills. They only numbed it and put me to sleep. When I woke up the pain was still there. It got so bad. I started losing sleep. I'd toss and turn all night. That's when I really learned to pray. Yes, God gives us doctors for a reason, but it doesn't stop at the doctor. It's not in the medicine or the hospitals. Prayer works faster than any procedure. It's never a wrong time to pray. I can remember a time when my husband was low on money. He stepped out on faith and quit his low paying job. We were out of food. People in America like to say that they are starving. We are spoiled. When you can go to the refrigerator and choose. You're not starving. Also, we can pull up at a drive-thru window and make a choice. We get to go grocery shopping and make a choice. There are people that don't have a choice. Some people have to drink the same water they bath in. Well, one day we were out of food. He went to work and I had been reading up on how a woman is supposed to keep the household. While he was at work, I did warfare in my apartment. I put on my praise music, and went to work. I began praying, and laying before God. I had heard the apostle speak about praying and listening. You not only have to pray, but stop to listen. Your answer may not come right then. I distinctly heard him tell me to dress my kitchen table like I was eating a big meal. You know me. I began to ask why. "I don't have any food to eat, so why am I looking stupid" God takes the foolish things to confound the wise. After setting the table there was more. Then he told me to take out my flour and meal, as if, I was baking or frying something. Then praise him like I already ate. I began praising Him and couldn't stop. In comes my husband with several bags of grocery. He said something about somebody owed him some money, or gave him some money. I really didn't care. Thanking God was my main priority. Some people say I could've called my mother or father for help. First, I knew He may not come when you want him, but He's always on time. I wanted to know if He did it all the time. Well, I got my answer. Second, I didn't want my husband to think I didn't trust him to be the head of the house. Third, I was determined to stick this out. I may not have been working, but I did my part. The way I looked at it was like this. If God keeps those who are faithful to him, then I need to be more faithful. I didn't become religious. My mind was made up and no one was stopping me. The spirit is willing, but the flesh is weak. The devil had to throw some stumbling blocks in my way. Let me give you a run down on what I'd already lost. I lost a chance to get my associates degree, my child's father, friends, cars, looks, money, a chance to have a normal body without seizures and strokes, eyesight, hair, and the ability to work. I lost all that, but I was determined not to lose my soul.

Forgive me. I may get carried away with my testimonies. So many things happened in my life. It's hard to keep track of when things occurred. Let me give you a few more testimonies. Then I'll tell you the last straw. I can remember a time when we lived in the four bed room apartment. There were church members living next door. This made me feel at ease, but no one could relate to my situation. I was trying hard to do right, but having diabetes is tricky. One night my blood sugar got really low. I was up stairs asleep. People don't understand. I tell them all the time. When your sugar level is too high or low you get delusional. Somehow, I got out of bed, made it down stairs, and no farther than the living room sofa. I guess I felt my sugar level had dropped and tried to make it to get something to eat. The next thing I know, the neighbors next door were in my house. My husband ran out to start the car. The first thing on my mind was natural. I was wondering why the neighbor was trying to put my clothes on. Then I realized it was actually happening. Then I realized my sugar level must have dropped too low. They checked it at home. It read LOW. It was so low that it didn't register on the machine. Once they rushed me to the hospital I began to cry. I thought about how young I was and going through so much brought tears to my eyes. My sugar level read 19. As the doctors worked on me, I began praising God. Another incident was similar. One morning I was seeing my son off to school. No one was at home because my husband still worked the morning shift. Well, I didn't know of the talking machines, yet. When my son would get up, I would always get him to read me what my machine would say. This morning we were running a little late. The bus pulled up and the machine went off. My son ran to the door without reading the machine, I yelled out for a reading, When he opened the door, he stuttered. As he went out the door, he said, "Five, five, and five." I went to the kitchen and fixed me some breakfast. Then I thought to myself. I shouldn't eat yet. I took enough insulin for five hundred and fifty five. I had no way of knowing it was the wrong reading. I couldn't see it. God was telling me to eat something then. When I took my insulin I put my food in the microwave oven. I walked up stairs and went to sleep. Once again, God woke me up. This I don't remember. I had gotten up out of the bed and tried to walk. I, somehow, fell in the middle of the floor. I must have hit my face. My lip was bleeding and I had a knot on my head. I don't know how long I was in the floor. My husband came home around three or three thirty. He found me in the middle of the floor with my eyes closed, rocking. He picked me up, threw me over his shoulders, carried me down stairs, and drove me to the hospital. Once I came to myself, I finally was told what happened. My son was in such a hurry, he repeated the number five too many times. It was actually, fifty five. When the doctors told me that I started to shout in my spirit. He had done it again. Not my husband but God. That's one reason God removed who he did. God is a jealous God. He doesn't want you to put anything or anyone before Him. I loved my husband. I was looking at the outer picture. I lost sight of the whole picture. I made him my big lord. I kind of forgot about the true and living God. One day he had come home and I had all the windows up. I didn't feel sick. The bible says that on your best day, you are sick enough to die. My husband got home and raced up stairs. The first thing he did was ask me what was wrong. He knew that I was anemic, but I had all the windows up. He rushed down to get my machine. He rushed out to get a ride, because my sugar level was too low. I started crying on the way to the hospital. I was upset over the things he had to go through. Then I thought about the scripture that says, "To whom much is given, much is required." That goes for both of us.

Now, this was the last straw for me. Things had been adding up. I would always try to shower him with gifts, but he was never happy. He would come up with these crazy excuses for coming in late. He all of a sudden, started to working after hours. I couldn't see, so I didn't worry about it. I've always had trust issues. I was determined to change my ways. I let it ride. One morning we had been into it over something. Not fighting. He all of a sudden he said he had to go. I pointed to the front door and asked him if he wanted me to help him pack. "No, I'm serious." I stopped, listened to the difference in his voice, and changed my tone quickly. "It hasn't gotten that bad. Has it? We can always talk about it." Then he started shaking his head. Once he told me that I just disgust him, I stopped walking, turned, and looked. All I saw was red. All fighters know what I mean. God instantly told me it's not worth it. Calmness came all over me. I picked up the telephone and called home. My mother answered the phone and I asked her if it was alright if we came home for a little while. She took her time and said, "You know you are always welcome to come home." After hanging up the phone, the devil came in. I began to think about all that I had lost. I ran up stairs, locked myself in the bath room, and started the water in the tub. No, I didn't wash it out; my whole purpose was to drown myself. He knocked on the door. I wouldn't answer. He burst through it and cut the water off. That morning I wanted to go visit my parents. He was on his way to work. The plans hadn't changed. On the way to Como, he reassured me it was only temporary. I got to my parents house and never told a soul. A day or two went by and I had to spill my guts. I, stupidly, reassured my mother we were just going through a rough spot. I'd learned to consult God before making a major move. I'd made up in my mind this wasn't over. I'm not going down without a fight. I called him every day. We went to the same church, so we tried being casual. That didn't work. No one said a word. Even though, I heard the whispering behind my back. I ignored it. One day I was at my grandmother's house visiting. As I sat on the porch, I dialed his cell phone number. Some female answered. I began to get stupid and blind. I instantly told myself that she must have been one of his nieces. Then I smiled and called back. Listening to all his dishonesty made me mad. I asked him, who was the lady that answered his phone. I don't remember what he said. Then I told him to be honest. "Are you still keeping your vows?" He took a little while to answer. After I heard no, my ears closed up. I slammed the phone down and began to cry. On the way home, my mother noticed the silence. When I began to get in the truck, I broke down. I couldn't take it anymore. My mother asked me what was wrong. "Nothing, I'm just getting a divorce." She was confused. I had been so determined and opened minded about the whole situation. Please, don't take the situation for face value. Look behind the broken vows, broken dreams, and broken promises. I have no regrets. It's better to have loved and lost than to have not loved at all.

Chapter 3

Divorce

Denial set in. Weeks and weeks had past. My dad was still driving my son to Batesville for school. My parents made the decision not to take him out in the middle of the school year. He was okay with that because he loved Batesville's school district. It took my youngest sister talking to me in a loving voice to see. We are usually direct and open. When her words are soft and slow God is using her. I started out hard and with a wall up, but she saw through that. It wasn't long before I started to break down. I was crying and I think she was too. I always thought wisdom was supposed to be displayed by the older sister or brother. This time it was the other way around. I made one more attempt to save my marriage. I asked my little sister if she would ride out with me. She knows what that means. She stopped and thought. "Not if you are going to do something crazy. You know I'm known to throw a homemade bomb in a minute. As slow as you walk we'll both be in jail. Then I'll have to leave you behind. Don't you call my name, because I'm going to act like I don't know you." she said. After taking my bath and putting on my clothes, I called to get directions to his new apartment. Please take in consideration; this was the same apartment I was waiting to move into. The same apartment he lived alone in. He gave me the apartment number and the directions to the apartment complex. The next thing he heard was me knocking at his front door. I should've known something by the way he answered the door. The first thing he did when he opened the door was look like a deer caught in head lights. He walked out and looked around. Then he asked me if anyone was with me. Next he wanted to know who brought me. I could tell he didn't want to let me in. I thought maybe he was dumb enough to have another female there. We talked, but I never got a definite answer. All he had to do was tell me it was over. Instead, he didn't sleep in the bed with me. He pulled a mattress off the bed and put it on the floor. I noticed he turned his back to me and never touched me. That gave me confirmation. The next day, he drove me home. I never looked back. All you holier than thou Christians are probably saying I should've stuck it out. Every marriage goes through its rough stage. Well, that's true. It also says in the bible that you have a right to a divorce when your husband or wife is not doing their duties as a mate. That happened a long time ago. No, it's not all about sex. This is how I felt. When we married I was his trophy wife. I became ill. He didn't look at me the same. I felt like a burden on him. Disabled or not, if you don't love that person, go. That's hurting that person more. People don't need eyes to see that. When I found out that every person has their breaking point. That was all I needed to know. You shouldn't have your limits with marriage or love. Correction, there should not be a limit with love. Marriage is a different thing. I clearly saw that he would string me along as long as I would go. I decided to put a period in that sentence. Don't get me wrong. I still love him, but I don't have passionate feelings for him. My love is Agapea love. There's a big difference. I could tell when he was going through something even though we were divorced. I could feel it in my spirit. It took me a while to let that go. It's like a parent and a child. Whenever the child is in distress, the parent will feel it. I struggled with dreams of him still sleeping in my bed. Then I had to face the fact that he would never touch or communicate with me again. God was trying to tell me to move on because he already had. The funniest thing about it was he used me to pay some move in bills. I was happy to help because I still viewed him as my husband. Besides, both of us were going to live in the place. I was clearly being used. I've moved on. He's history.

The Broken Promises

You said you'd love and charish me
Until death do us part
You said you'd not only share your mind and
money,
But also your heart
You promised me your body was mine
I guess certain parts had a mind of their own
I heard the many lies you told,
But that's okay
Being with you made me bold
From wearing my heart on my shirt sleeve
To laying down with dogs,
And getting fleas
Some trials and tribulations break you
If you let them
These made me be a stronger me
I hope you asked for forgiveness
For the simple promises you broke
Everybody knows it's better not to make a vow with God
Than to make one and break it
Smile
Because the first book is dedicated to you
The next one will be for someone new

Chapter 4

Illness

WARNING! WARNING! WARNING! WHY DIDN'T anyone tell me I would feel this way when I returned home? The four walls were beginning to close in. I cried all through the night. I cried when people were not in the room. I cried when I ate. Well, when they forced me to eat. Food didn't taste like food anymore. Then my little guardian angel stepped in. My son came to me and asked if I was still sick. People may say I give my son a little too much credit. No, there are many times I've heard the voice of God through my son. Remember, God has no respective person. He can use anyone. The word of God can come from a child, woman, sinner, or a dying person. Take heed when it does. That woke me up. Even though it seemed like my world had ended. I still had a son to raise. I never stopped going to church. Do you know you can still be going to church and back slide? I had back slid in my heart. I would sit in church and it seemed like the preacher was speaking a foreign language. Then I got like most people going through something. The word came across the pulpit. It sounded like they were picking on me. First, rage came. Second, the old me was back. I did things the way I wanted to do them. I had just as much sense as others.

Third, I was in the process of moving my membership. After thinking long and hard about the situation, I had a visit by my little sister. Her words were hard and harsh, but they were real. After giving me a few of her testimonies, I felt like I could run just a little farther, In my talk with my little sister, I learned other people have been through just as much as me. Everyone doesn't shut down and cry a river of tears. Crying is fine. Have your little moment of crying, suck it up, and make a new strategy. I slung my heart over my shoulder with a chain, picked up my cross, and returned to church. It wasn't easy. I had to use a chain for my heart. It was now heavy. It felt like it was an anchor attached to a ship. I went in with a smile, but was crying all along. One night I read in the word something that helped me smile with sincerity. The word says that if you sow in tears. You shall reap in joy. That's why my favorite scripture in the bible is: The race is not given to the swift nor the battle to the strong, but to the one who endureth to the end. I kept going to church, smiling, and acting like nothing really mattered. Soon my husband became my ex husband. I wasn't out of the wilderness. My previous husband motivated me to go back to school and write a book. Of course, I was blind, so I had to enroll in a school for the seeing impaired. The best college was out of Jackson, MS. They denied me because of my health. I don't know whether it was me or my mom that was more determined. We tried a college in Tupelo, MS. Before that even happened, I took a turn for the worse. I had never gone through a seizure. I remember like it was yesterday. I was on my way home from dialysis treatment. Just as we reached the road to my house, I had this jerk in my body that was unusual. Instantly, I announced to the driver that I was about to have a seizure. The next thing I remember is waking up in the yard. My dad, the Medicaid driver, and the EMT driver were trying to wake me. It took the doctors a while to establish the dosage of my medicine. People told me that I wasn't having seizures because my seizures weren't the same as others. I had to have been misdiagnosed. It happened again and at the same place. This time it was a different driver. She got me home just in time. I still ended up having the seizure. After going through this over and over, God gave me wisdom. I told my mom how I noticed the atmosphere my pastor's family made when she had a seizure. Her mom kept calling her name in a calm manor. I remember asking her why she did that. She told me my pastor recognizes the sound of her voice. It calms her down and makes her take control of the seizure. I remember walking to the truck with my mother. I could tell when I was having a seizure. I called out to my mother. She began to calmly coach me through it. One or two times that would happen. Then I would have a major seizure. Not only was I having seizures. I was in a new place, so I had to get use to the rooms and steps. I would fall in a minute. It happened so much. They stopped rushing me off to the hospital. My memory would get bad sometimes. I would tell my mother that something wasn't right. Because she had so much going on, she would brush it off. Once it got too bad, she took me to the hospital. The doctors couldn't tell me what happened. This kept reoccurring. This time I would be lying in the bed and I would feel the bed moving. I would end up in the middle of the bed, sideways or on the floor. My mother left her door opened so she could see. She would be so tired from work. I began to get on her nerves. As she would come through the doors yelling about sleep, I had enough sense to tell myself something wasn't right. Finally, I got to the hospital. My leg had started moving involuntarily. It was embarrassing but this was something I couldn't control. Besides the diabetes, high blood pressure, seizures, and no eyesight. I had gone through a stroke. People were wondering why God wouldn't stay out of my mouth. One reason was because He was still blessing. I was going through things, but He brought me through. A lot of people don't live to tell the story. Going back and forth to dialysis caused my blood pressure to rise. I constantly had a high blood pressure. At times, my head would hurt extremely bad. At times, it would last for days. One time it was hurting so bad. My parents took me to Oxford. They checked my blood pressure. It was at stroke level. That wasn't something new. It wasn't just one hundred and something over one hundred and something. It was in the two hundred range. They ran more tests. We were wondering why they were keeping me so long. Usually, they give me a blood pressure pill, and it stabilizes it. I know the reason why it took doctors so long to bring me the results back. They were wondering how could this happen. God works in mysterious ways. He can bless who He wants to bless. The doctors came in and checked my blood pressure again. It had started to go down. That was the good news. The bad news was I had an aneurism in the brain. I'd never heard of an aneurism. I'm blind, but I could see that the doctors were shocked. They wanted to know how I could still be walking around after having an aneurism. They actually said it stopped before spreading farther. Another serious moment happened at my parent's house. My mother and I were at the library in the town. We were leaving because it was time for her to go to work. The truck wouldn't start. She saw a friend of hers. The lady agreed to take us home. As I got out of my mother's vehicle, she noticed my clothes were slightly bloody. My mother tried putting something over the seat as we road home. I changed clothes once I got home. Then she left for work. My son's aunt Tarsha brought him home from school. We were talking, casually, for a while. When I arose to go to the bath room, she noticed I was sitting in a puddle of blood. By this time, I figured God made my menstrual cycle begin again. From the time I began dialysis, my menstrual cycle had ceased. To the bath room I went. Tarsha stood and talked to me through the bathroom door. While using the bathroom the bottom fell out, again. This time I began to get scared. Tarsha asked if she could help. Being as cautious as I am about people seeing me naked, I requested that she go get the telephone so I could call my mother. As bad as she wanted to stay at work she left. My mother suggested me to call 9 1 1 and she would meet me at the hospital. Of course, I refused. I've had doctors and nurses give me the wrong medicine when she wasn't there. I waited on her. Tarsha was kind enough to wait with me. My mother drove me to Oxford. To be honest, I thought I was dying. As I changed my clothes for the third time, I repented for all my sins. Well, you know they kept me in Oxford. The workers at the hospital had seen me so many times. They knew me by heart. It made me feel good, but bad at the same time. Once I woke up from all the pain medicine. A doctor came in and told me I had an ulcer. No one explained to me how a person gets an ulcer. He informed me there would be a procedure in the morning. I had to have a surgery on my colon. My first question was if I would be sedated or not. He reassured me I would be sedated and wouldn't feel a thing. Once the procedure was over, the same doctor came to talk to me. Like most doctors, he was shocked. He told me he knows I had an ulcer. The only thing is we know it's in your stomach, but our machines can't find the hole. He informed me there would be another procedure to make sure it doesn't happen again. That day another procedure was done. The same doctor held another conversation with me. The machines are up to date, but they still couldn't find anything. They weren't going to give me the medicine. He stated that he didn't understand it. I said, "I know exactly what happened. It was God." He thought I was crazy. He walked out mumbling something to himself. See, doctors think it's all about them and the machine or the procedure. God can simply touch one spot and heal it all. People may look at me crazy, and treat me funny. I may even have people that think I shouldn't receive some of the things I get. I had to realize God gave me favor a long time ago. The funny thing about it, favor is not fair. The lowest person you may think is nothing. God is looking at it differently. The word says that the first shall be last, and the last shall be first. So, keep on putting me to the end of the line, and sniffing your nose up at my situation. Please, don't talk about me. God will take the very thing I deal with, and put it on you.

Please, don't think I woke up one morning and was grateful for all my trials and tribulations. God had to bring this time back to my mind. I remember asking God why I had to go through all this pain. He let me know I was going through my Job syndrome. If I go through, not complaining and believing, he will bring me through it all. I'll have an award at the end. Then I told God that I would go through if it was for his name sake. Going through just to be going through is one thing. Going through to get God's glory out of your life is another. I can remember hearing people stand in church and say or speak of spirits they saw. I thought that was neat. I asked God if He would bless me with that gift. I could tell when a person had a spirit, but couldn't see them spiritually. One night my son and I were home alone. My husband was at work. I had got up to get some water out of the refrigerator. As I closed the door, and poured the water, I walked back. Just as I closed the door of the refrigerator, a tall man walked out. He was dressed in a basketball out fit. I was in my flesh, so it terrified me. I never said anything. I sat on my sofa, as my son watched television on the floor. I thought of no one to call. Then as I sat there three more people came to the passage way from the living room to the kitchen. I immediately picked up the telephone and called my pastor. She began to laugh. At that time, I didn't think it was all that funny. I was sitting on the sofa going crazy. It alarmed my son. He got up in tears and began to reassure me there was nothing there. It had to scare him, because he wouldn't go to bed. We both stayed on the sofa until my ex husband came home. Seeing spirits was one thing, but the devil began to make me look delusional. My son and pastor calmed my nerves, and I layed back down. Remember, I'm still blind. I happened to open my eyes. Just in time to see this "It" like character walk across my floor. Once again, I called my pastor. I explained to her that the character looked like "It" on the monsters. Its hair was all over its head and it walked slowly. Once again, she laughed. I don't think my situation was making her laugh. I think it was the sound of my voice. I love to act. I am capable of being a drama queen. It got worse and worse over the next few days. One night we were going to bed. My hair was braided. As I layed down, I could see braid like figures going under my pillow. I know that sounds crazy, so I never said a word. It didn't just stop there. The braids started binding me up. I jumped up out of the bed and screamed. My husband didn't know what to do. I don't remember how, but they took me to the hospital. When the problem is too big for Tri Lakes they'll ship you off to Oxford. I didn't stay there too long. My husband came to Oxford right after I got there. Remember, I'm still blind. I was telling my husband I could see the wall. I told him what color it was. Then a doctor came in and told me I was going to be admitted in Tupelo's hospital. No one had to explain it to me. I knew it must have been too severe.

When the EMT came to get me, it was raining. Once they had me in the ambulance it became extreme. The EMT worker was sitting at the back evaluating me. He must have been experienced with that sort of thing. He never lost his cool. As I was laying there being evaluated, the enemy started to play with my mind. I heard some noise. I looked to the right and saw three small alligators. At first, they were about five inches away. I didn't want anyone to think I was crazy, so I said nothing. Then the alligators came closer. They were so close I could feel them gnawing at me. I leaned over to my left. The EMT worker asked me what was wrong. I told him what it was. He didn't laugh. He looked long and searched hard, but found nothing. Then he reassured me there was nothing there. Then he said there was something wrong. He said he thought I'd experienced a lot in the past few years. I was just over come by them. I don't understand why it hadn't happened before now. They admitted me in the hospital, and everything was cool for a while. Then the door was opened and the devil stepped in. Later on in the night, things started to crawl on me. I had spiders, rats, dogs, and something in my food. It got so bad. I was calling the nurse so much until they placed me behind the nurse's station. This was my second day there. I'd begun to look like I should be locked up in a nut house. Even though I couldn't see, I could hear all the whispering about me. At this time, the little spiders turned into huge ones. I was jumping and jerking. A doctor had to come in and give me medicine by IV and mouth. It took a while for it to take effect, and I was on the call button every minute. In the meanwhile, a chaplain came by. She brought my mind back into focus. She started reminding me who I was, and who I served. She reminded me to rest in Jesus. There was nothing the devil could do. It was only fear that was taking over. Then I thought about it. All the things that had me on edge were things I was scared of. She asked me if I sing. I said, "Yes, we do a lot of singing at my church." She told me when she's going through something singing calms her nerves. It's only the word of God put in the form of a song. I agreed with her, and she began to sing. All the huge spiders in my head began to fall. I felt better, but she had to move on. They came back as soon as she left. My husband said he was on his way, and I was rushing him. I was almost about to jump out of my skin when he got there. He wanted to take my mind off all that. I guess he thought it was the room. We decided to go for a walk down the hall. I enjoyed it. Once we were back it started again. God was showing me what I needed to do. Fear had taken over, and I was at a standstill. I could remember my pastor just telling me it was my time. I got so mad. Then God had to reveal to me what was going on. I had gotten use to my pastor taking me by my hands and babying me. God sent me one more person. My favorite person. My little sister came with my mother and father. While they were there in awe. She rolled up her sleeves and went to work. She let me know that I wasn't alone. She told me how she went through something similar. When my family left, I had another rough night. My head was opened to the fact that none of this was real. I knew how powerful prayer was. I was so scared of looking or seeming crazy. The enemy had a field day with my fear. They put me on seroquel. That medicine is the type of medicine you can't wing yourself off of. I would notice what would happen when I missed a few pills. I would see things. Even though my mind was perfectly fine, I remained on the medicine. One night when I was in warfare at home, I can remember pleading out for God to deliver me from this medicine. I let Him know there was no way I could do it alone. He had to help. I am now thinking back before moving home. I had a particular incident. I was at dialysis. It was time to go. The Medicaid driver came in to get me. He was rolling me out to the van. There was a man standing at the window looking out. He was tall, dark, and never said a word. He turned as we came from the lobby into another part of the building. Before we made it to the other door, he turned as if he was waiting specifically for me. He didn't have an awful face. One of those faces that scares others. He walked right into me. I was being rolled out in a wheel chair. He was standing there as I made it to the van. He then turned and walked into me again. I asked the driver if he saw that. He asked me what? I explained. He really thought I had lost my mind. He left to go get the charge nurse. She came out and asked me if I was okay. I calmed down and got inside. That same guy was sitting there waiting on me. Another mean faced guy got in behind me. He was short and didn't look like an angel. When the driver took me to the apartment they were standing at my door when I got home. They would already be there whenever I would sit or stand. I had begun to take a lot of tests to have my name placed on the kidney transplant list. I had taken a pap smear. That test came back normal, but the breast exam wasn't. I was sent to take a mammogram. I thought it was just an x-ray of your breast. Wrong! After that, they have to send you the results. It seems like it takes very little to get negative results. They called me to schedule an appointment. I went in scared, but depending on God. The only frightening part about it was that my mom couldn't be in the room with me. As I layed there on the table, cold as I could be, all kind of thoughts ran through my head. When the doctor walked in about twelve men followed. They were dressed in lab coats. They were tall and handsome. They all lined up before me. I think because I was in such shock, I didn't feel a thing. When it was over I opened my eyes and they were all gone. I don't think I ever told anyone until I knew what really was going on. I knew the type of church I was in. The world, itself, doesn't believe in spiritual things like witches, demons, devils, spells, curses, generational curses, spiritual gifts, prophecy, or apostles. I'd learned not to tell people not of the same faith. They wouldn't understand. One day the apostle was ministering to me. He wanted to let me know God was showing me my personal guardian angels that were watching over me. He also asked me why I didn't talk to those people standing in my house. I laughed in fear. Sometimes, we ask God for certain blessings, but can you handle the blessing? Later, God delivered me from seroquel. It was weeks before I knew. I thanked God once I found out. I knew I couldn't do it by myself. Things that are impossible with man are possible with God which brings me to my next testimony. I'd been taking treatment for my kidneys for six years. During the process, I had some near death experiences. One morning while waiting to go to the back for treatment, Mrs. Webb started to talk to me. I liked her so I conversed back. She asked me if I was told about yesterday's incident. I asked her what happened. She told me I wasn't responsive while waiting to go home. I asked her what they did. She told me they put me in the middle of the floor and did CPR on me. That shocked me. I knew then I had to pray every time I stepped foot in the doors. Then there was this time I was on my way home. A nurse named Katrina was bandaging my arm for me. She was doing just fine until she got some calls on her cell phone. Notice I said some calls. I'm a hard person to stop from bleeding, so nurses have to take their time with me. Sometimes they would hold my arm in place for over an hour. This day she got calls after calls. I can truly say she wasn't paying attention. Before she let me go we had an accident. She then had to hang up her phone and wipe up blood. Again, she started talking on the cell phone. She tried it again. I never thought about it. Before the van could leave she was called out to bandage me again. I was so tired. I was just glad to get home. My little sister was leaving when I got home. We greeted one another and she left. My butt didn't get warm before I started bleeding again. I took my coat off, and my son saw it. I remained calm so I wouldn't scare him. Then I told him all he had to do was go get a small towel. That didn't work. He started getting alarmed when he saw that the blood kept flowing. I told him to just get a bigger towel. I didn't want to upset anyone, because they would upset me. Just as my son layed the big towel on my arm, my dad stepped to the door. He asked, in a loud voice, "What's wrong!" He was running around in a circle. I told someone to call my little sister back. She was on her way to Memphis. I knew she would know what to do, because she was a phlebotomist. She rushed home and into the house. The first thing out of her mouth was let's go to the hospital. I wined like a baby. She angrily said it wasn't about my fear. It was about my life. "Get your *** up and let's go!" she yelled. She did over a hundred on the interstate. She called the ER and warned them she was bringing me in. She kept me alert and talking. Once we drove up to the hospital I began to go out. They got me out and put me in a wheel chair. I had lost so much blood. I'm surprised Eve didn't act a nut over her bloody seat. I could hear everything going on. They tried to find a vein but wasn't successful. Then they had to put a pick line in my neck. At that point, I could've jumped up and walked out. Once they got the pick line in my mother walked in. They told her that I was going on a helicopter. They just needed her consent. I began to get scared. It was only one or two seconds and they gave me some medicine to knock me out. Correction, it wasn't a pick line. It was a central line in my neck. I could have treatment, draw blood, and get pain medicine from this line. I never knew where I was. All I heard was that I had lost five pints of blood. They also had to stitch my arm up. My next testimony makes me dance every time I think about it. I never get tired of telling it. My pastor and the apostle went out of town, so they left one of our member's named Switzerland Bonner to preach. She always gives a good message. After giving the message, she called all ministers to the alter for prayer. I slowly walked up. Everyone knows I have a problem standing. Give me time. God is working on it. A deacon brought me a chair to sit in. We've been taught not to wait for someone to lay hands on you. Get it for yourself. I began to pray. After a while, I got caught up in spiritual tongs. Ms. Bonner came over and asked me if anyone had prayed for me, yet? Then she started to minister. She said that I have faith, but God says give him more. "I know you're saying I have more than enough faith. God says when you give him a little more he'll do that thing you thought he couldn't do." she said. I walked away confused as ever. All that day Sunday service stayed on my mind. It was late at night, and I was ready to go to bed. I had just told my mother that I was getting ready to go to bed. My mother laughed because it was early for me. Just as I stood up to go to bed, the telephone rang. I sat back down. The lady on the telephone told me her name. Then she told me where she was calling me from. Once I heard kidney transplant hospital, my mind had a lot of questions. First, I was wondering why she had to call me at this time. Couldn't they call people during office hours? Second, I thought my next appointment was months away. Third, what hoop did they want me to jump through, now? When she said she was calling me to let me know that they had a kidney for me, my ears instantly closed down. The lady was talking to herself. I heard nothing else she said. I had sat down and started to dance sitting down. My mom saw that it must have been good news, so she sat beside me. I had to interrupt the lady to tell her she had to talk to my mother. I reminded her that I was blind. Then I said I was about to do a holy dance in the middle of the floor with my son. We danced so. I must have been on cloud 99. They only give you so much time to get there. I've never seen my family get ready so quickly. I prayed on the way to Memphis. I really got scared sitting in the waiting room. It took them so long to work me up. Once I was in the room, I had to be prepped for surgery. My son played my favorite song while I layed in bed, shaking. They told me they would give me medicine to put me to sleep. They were running behind time. The medicine never came, so I got worried. I prayed before surgery, and gave my son the talk of life. I've given that talk so many times. I guess my son wants to know why it keeps changing. Just before we went to have surgery, I had to have another treatment. See, the day they scheduled surgery was my treatment day. I, obviously, had too much fluid on my body to have surgery. I began to get upset when they ordered me to take a treatment first. Usually, I would numb my arm. At that point, I started freaking out. Then God had to instantly tell me that was the last time. Whoever was looking at me must have thought I was crazy. I stopped freaking out and came back with a smile. I thought I would be in a room alone. It sounded like someone else was there. This person was waking up from surgery. They had me lying there so long. I fell asleep, but I let them know I hadn't received the anesthesia. They laughed. Once again, I felt that icky feeling. The surgery lasted for hours, but seemed like minutes. My mother's whole side of her family was there. The whole family stood and prayed for me when I came out. They would've put me in my regular room, but it was too small for the family. When I came to myself I could name everyone standing in the room. Even though I am blind, I have hearing out of this world. My oldest uncle is a chaplain at this transplant hospital. He was in my room. I couldn't see it, but I knew something different was going on with my neck. I forgot that they had to put a central line in my neck. I can remember him grabbing my hands. He told me later I was trying my best to yank the IV out. The day of my surgery a few of my family members stayed over. My mother's only sister was there holding my hand. After surgery, there was so much pain. On the way to the restroom, it was painful as I got up. I used the restroom before they put a catheter in. I struggled to use it. When I came out my mother reached for my hand, I snapped before I knew it. I said, "Don't touch me. I'm in too much pain." I must have hurt her feelings because my dad mentioned it to me, later. I instantly called her to apologize. I'm just that crazy for God. I thought He had done it all. Someone had to tell me I still was blind. No, my cheese didn't slip off its cracker. My knees buckled as my feet hit the floor. At this time, my uncle Verny was visiting from Florida. He's out of this world funny. A few sisters and brothers, on my dad's side, have a speech impediment. I'm not laughing at that. He tells a lot of jokes and you can't laugh because you don't understand him. He and my son had me busting a gut while I stayed in the hospital. I had the surgery on Tuesday. By Saturday afternoon I was at home. My kidney hasn't given me any problems. I remember asking one of the nurses if all the patients went home this soon. She said, "No, some patients have to stay from two to four months. You are doing just fine. The little pain you going through, now, is to be expected." The only problem is getting my anti rejection medicine corrected. The doctors are so precise. I was under doctor's care for three months. For three months I wasn't supposed to leave the house. Well, we had a family vacation in Hot Springs Arkansas. Even though they specifically told me my immune system hadn't built up, I was determined to go have fun somewhere and not be rushed back for kidney treatment. I felt fine when I got back. My mother and son were going on a cruise in a week. My daddy demanded my mother to stay, but I realized she has always put her life on hold for me. Then too, my son has never enjoyed being a normal child. I begged her to go. She left my aunt Rachael in charge. At this time, I lost so much weight. I got sick. Pants that were tight on me, suddenly, became too big. Even a belt didn't help. I don't remember what the reason was, but I had to be admitted in the hospital. Yes, I know. My sugar level was staying too high. It was from 500 to

599. They informed me that if my sugar level stayed that high, I was risking damaging my new kidney. All I was worried about was my daddy. The doctors let him know it happens to everyone. The anti rejection medicine had to be adjusted. Something could be too high or too low. Even though I was admitted in the hospital, that made me feel good. Once I got out the hospital, I struggled with my weight. It took me forever to gain weight. As soon as I would gain a pound, I would lose it. Gaining weight from 90 pounds to 100 pounds was a big hurdle to jump. Giving all glory to God, we did it.

Chapter 5

Restoration

RESTORATION DOESN'T ALWAYS MEAN PUTTING things back the way they were prior to an event or circumstance. I was restored into what God wants me to be. I guess you're probably asking, "How can you be restored into something you've never been?" Well, I have always been a woman of God. I've just never walked in my anointing. What people don't understand is that God is not asking you to walk like this person. He's not asking you to talk like that person. All God is asking of you is to confess it with your mouth that Jesus died for our sins and He is your Lord and savior. He wants you to repent and live saved to the best of your ability. Everyone thinks that God is mean. God is a graceful and merciful God. Let's just thank Him for not being the way he used to be. Back in the biblical days, if you sinned, God automatically struck you dead. That was before Jesus stepped on the scene. When Jesus came, He was the mediator. He is someone that stands in the gap for you and I. Someone that can plead your case for you. When you sin, God is ready to take you out, but Jesus steps in and begs God to give you another chance. Before going to God you must come to Jesus. That's the proper operation. If you don't believe me, do me a favor and read your word for yourself. In reading Proverbs, you see it says, "Trust in the Lord in all your ways. Lean not on your own understanding, and He will direct your ways." That means you pray for wisdom and knowledge. You can't trust the words of a preacher anymore. They'll lie to you just like anyone else.

Being restored doesn't happen overnight. I have to deal with that now. People want everything micro waved. They don't have time to let it cook and simmer. If you go slow, and give God time to do his job, you can't go wrong. Like with my kidney and school, I told you I am a dreamer. God gives me dreams on whom or what I should pray for. He lets me know how I should minister. I'm not fluent in prophecy, but I know it's there. Everyone wants the gifts, but can you go through what it takes to be anointed. It's not all about the gifts. God says that all you have to do is ask for it. I really just want my soul to be saved. I want to keep my salvation. One night I had a dream. I was driving a car. Jesus was on the passenger side. I was going in pot holes, riding through rivers, falling off cliffs, and going through dark tunnels. I looked over and Jesus said, "The ride will be much smoother if you let me drive." I had to make sure I heard Him correctly. So, I said, "What?" He repeated and spoke a little louder. "Once you get out of the driver's seat, let me drive, and sit over here and ride it out, the ride will be much smoother. I got this one." At that time, I decided to wait on school. I thought to myself. If they give me a certain amount of time to get to the hospital and I am not there they'll skip right on past my name. They will move on to the next person who wants the kidney worse than I do. I figured six years was a little too long for me. The drive from the school was too long. I called the recruiter and put school off for a while. She didn't understand, my son didn't understand, friends didn't understand, and family didn't try to understand. It really didn't matter to me. I knew what God had told me. One morning I was lying in bed. The telephone rang. I sleep right by the telephone, so you know I heard it. Usually, my daddy won't wake me up when I'm asleep. He believes in getting your rest. I heard him clearly. He answered the phone and said, "Here she is right here." All I could say in my head was,

"I know he sees me asleep." Anyway, as I layed there, she began to talk. She told me her name. I couldn't tell you who I talked to this day. After she told me she was from the eye transplant hospital in Florida. I rose up. I wanted to make sure I wasn't asleep. I sat up on the side of the bed. She asked if I was blind. She wanted to know how blind. I laughed and said, "Can't see anything, blind." Then she wanted to know a little more. She wanted to know if I had time to answer a few questions. I was shocked to get the telephone call. I answered every question quickly. She wanted to know how much income was made in the household. Once I told her she told me I was approved for the help. I began to shout in my spirit. She said in a month I would receive a letter from Hamilton Eye Clinic. They would be writing me to give me directions to the place in Florida. She let me know I would get that letter in a month. A month came and went. Being as excited as I was, I called Florida. The lady I talked to wasn't professional. She got loud and irate with me. She told me I was confused and mistaken. I broke it all down to her. She still informed me I was crazy. I've learned it doesn't help to get on their level of stupidity. I calmly asked her if I could speak to someone in higher authority than her. With a loud voice she shouts, "There is no one else." I in return said to her, "No mam, I mean someone you have to answer to." She put me on hold and quickly clicked back over. Then said," She said to tell you that we don't give a whole eye transplant. We send the corrective tissue." I said with tears in my eyes, "Thank you, mam, and you have a blessed day." I didn't take hours rolling in the middle of the floor. I didn't empty a box of Kleenex. I simply wiped my eyes, smiled, and repeated something the apostle taught me. I said, "All is well." Not letting it rest, I asked my dad if he could remember me getting a telephone call from Florida. He said, "Yes, because I stood right here and listened to your whole conversation." Then I had a little talk with God. I can remember saying, "I don't know if you're letting me know I won't receive my sight from a transplant but a miracle. I guess the only way I'll get my eyes is coming straight from you." Then I had to correct that. I knew that he would do it all. Everyone thinks the miracle comes from the doctors and the machines.

But, without God, where would you be? God has to touch the body of that doctor or the mechanics of the machine. Wrong! Anything made or designed by man is capable of failing. God knows all and makes no mistakes. It's funny, but today is January 14, 2011. I just received a call while typing on this book. Guess who it was? It was The Hamilton Clinic from Memphis, TN. I almost missed the call. When I am typing, I won't move. That means answering the telephone, door, or eating. I will wait to the last minute to use the bathroom. Anyway, the telephone rang for at least twenty times. I, finally, got up to answer. When I answered, there was no one there. I clicked over and I heard a voice. She let me know who she was and where she was calling from. It made me smile because I was just typing about the disappointment I had. She asked if I had put in an application with them. I was lost, so she refreshed my memory. Once we agreed I had applied for service, she asked how many surgeries have I had? After telling her I've had more than I can count on one hand. Then she asked if anyone ever told me there was nothing they could do. I responded by saying, "No, they really never told me anything." So, it's really not an emergency." I corrected her. "Yes it is an emergency. I have a son to raise and I want to enjoy my life." The conversation was short and sweet. She let me know that the Hamilton Clinic would be writing me a letter. In this letter it would contain the directions, date, and time of my appointment. She also apologized for the delay. I told her that I thought something was wrong because I was looking for the letter a month ago. After we talked, I ran to my mother to let her know. Once my dad was in the house, she told him. He then said the same exact thing God has been telling me. You can't rush God. He's going to bless you when he gets ready. No sooner. Stop telling people and tell God. As much as I hated to, I agreed with him. Restoration doesn't happen overnight. It doesn't just fall from the sky. Faith without works is dead. You can't just say I want to be healed or restored. There must be some work involved. In other words, you have to labor for it. Don't get me wrong. There's going to be talk. In my process, I had to be delivered from people. People always want to put their two cents in. You're the one going through that situation. You have to want it just that bad; bad enough to shut everybody's mouth up. My oldest sister said something years ago. I was mad and upset over something. She turned and said, "Get mad! I hope you're mad enough to do something about it!" She doesn't know. I use that to this very day.

In conclusion, the purpose of the whole book is simple. I didn't write all this to take the scab off old wounds. Marshell wants you to know that you, too, are an over comer. Healing, blessings, miracles, faith, and restoration don't come over night. There must be labor involved. You have to work for it. You can have all the faith in the world. If you don't get up off your do nothing and work for it, it won't happen. It takes praying, reading, praise, and laying before God for his guidance. First and far most, you must fast. Fasting doesn't always mean you go without eating. You can fast from whatever you love too much. A fast is simply putting away something to offer yourself to God. By offering yourself to God, you don't do anything to damage the temple. You do know your body is a temple. Then you can't just starve yourself of something. You have to do without things you love, and replace it with the word of God. Anything you feed will grow or get bigger. Feeding your natural man or body will make your fleshly body get stronger or grow. Feeding your spiritual man will make your spiritual man grow or get stronger. Trust me, God understands. Fasts don't have to last for days or hours. You can start out slow. God gives everyone a measure of faith. Don't fret. Your faith just hasn't gotten there yet. Ask God for it.

There are so many people walking around with no clue. They were told there is a God, but they don't believe in death or hell. Get real! Then I've talked to people who ask me, "Why do I believe in all that stuff?" Why not? I'd rather believe in something helping me. Than believe in nothing and go straight to hell. Please, let me take the time to clarify a few things before departing. This book was only written to glorify God. Yes, I still love my ex husband. Not in a passionate way. I love myself and my son too much to be unhappy my whole life. I've learned to love everyone. I may hate your ways, but it's nothing against you. "Testimonies" was written simply for glory. If anyone was hurt in the process, please, do like I've done my whole life. Take a lick and keep on ticking. Do me a favor. Please, you forgive me, so God can forgive you.

Surviver

I open my eyes,
And begin to scream
Once again, I close and open them,
And I still can't see
Moments later, I find myself
In the middle of the floor
Screaming
"Help Me! Help Me!
Vision is at my fingertip
But I can't grabb it"
My ears stood to atention
Like an antanna on an automotive vehicle
HE SPOKE SO CLEARLY
"It's already done
I've placed in you things to help you be FREE
You are a Praiser, an Overcomer, a prayer
worrior, and a demon killer,
But most of all
You are a SURVIVER
A surviver doesn't take no for an answer
A surviver won't roll over for anyone
A surviver stairs the enemy in the face
With tears running like a rushing river, and smiles
While the entire world is rolling on smoothly
A surviver goes through many tribulations and trials
Knowing that these words are true
1 John 4:4 Ye are of God little children, and have overcome them;
because greater is he that is in you, than he
that is in the world.

Words of Thanks and Dedication

I want to thank God. Without him none of this would be possible. I thank my son, Timothy T. Corner, Jr., My family, friends, and spiritual family too. I dedicate this book to Vanessa S. Conner, Willie T. Harmon, Timothy T. Corner Sr., Charo Davis-Jefferson, the Taylor family, Ms. Switzerland Bonner, and the Thompson family for pushing me to do my very best. I had to let people know that I serve a God that makes the last first. Unlike man, He never forsakes you. May God bless and keep you. This one is for you.

BACKGROUND HISTORY

Ms. Marshell Wortham was born July 7, 1977. She was born in Memphis, TN at The Med. She is originally from Clarksdale, MS. At a very young age she moved to Senatobia, MS. She now resides in Como; MS. Marshell is divorced and single with one son, Timothy T. Corner. Next to God, he's her world.